family favorites

Home-style heart warming recipes

This edition published in 2012

LOVE FOOD is an imprint of Parragon Books Ltd

Parragon
Queen Street House
4 Queen Street
Bath BA1 1HE, UK

Copyright © Parragon Books Ltd 2011

LOVE FOOD and the accompanying heart device is a registered trademark
of Parragon Books Ltd in Australia, the UK, USA, India, and the EU.

www.parragon.com

ISBN: 978-1-4454-4051-4

Printed in China

Notes for the Reader
This book uses standard kitchen measuring spoons and cups. All spoon
and cup measurements are level unless otherwise indicated. Unless
otherwise stated, milk is assumed to be whole, eggs are large, individual
vegetables are medium, and pepper is freshly ground black pepper.

The times given are only an approximate guide. Preparation times differ
according to the techniques used by different people and the cooking times
may also vary from those given. Optional ingredients, variations, or serving
suggestions have not been included in the calculations.

Recipes using raw or very lightly cooked eggs should be avoided by infants,
the elderly, pregnant women, convalescents, and anyone with a chronic
illness. Pregnant and breast-feeding women are advised to avoid eating
peanuts and peanut products. People with nut allergies should be aware
that some of the prepared ingredients used in the recipes in this book may
contain nuts. Always check the packaging before use.

contents

introduction

This collection of mouthwatering soups, stews, chilis and hearty meals reflects the country's great culinary history, focusing on a broad range of classic homemade dishes.

Here is a colorful range of soups, and chowders from *Cream of Mushroom Soup*, and *Cream of Tomato Soup*, to *Corn and Clam Chowder* and *Lobster Bisque.*

Central to any collection are meat stews (*Hearty Beef Stew* and *Chile Verde Pork Stew*,) chicken-based favorites (*Chicken and Mushroom Marsala* and *Old-Fashioned Chicken and Dumplings*,) and spicy chilis (*Firehouse Chili Con Carne*, and *Chicken and White Bean Chili*.) Also, regional favorites from *Yankee Pot Roast* to *San Francisco Cioppino*, and *King Ranch Chicken Casserole* from Texas add more colors and flavors.

No cookbook would be complete without a few carefully selected side dishes, so several ideal accompaniments, such as *Boston Baked Beans*, *Creamy Corn Custard*, and *Cornbread* complete the collection.

With beautiful color photographs illustrating each recipe, this is a book every home cook, beginner or experienced, will want on their shelf and will turn to for decades for inspiration and support.

everday soups and chowders

cream of tomato soup

Rumor has it this easy soup goes really, really great with grilled cheese sandwiches.

serves 6

2 tablespoons unsalted butter

1 medium sweet onion, coarsely chopped

Salt

1 (28-ounce) can whole, peeled, Italian plum tomatoes

1 clove garlic, halved

2 cups chicken broth

½ cup water

1 teaspoon sugar

1 bay leaf

½ cup heavy cream

Freshly ground black pepper to taste

1 tablespoon freshly sliced chives

Melt butter in a saucepan over medium heat. Add the onion with a pinch of salt. Cook, stirring occasionally, for about 10 to 12 minutes until the onion is soft and golden. Add tomatoes (do not drain) to the saucepan and use a wooden spoon, or potato masher to break into large chunks. Add the garlic, chicken broth, water, sugar, and bay leaf; bring to a simmer. Simmer for 30 minutes.

Remove from heat, and take out the bay leaf. Carefully puree the soup in small batches in a blender until very smooth. Strain the soup back into the saucepan; place over medium-low heat, and bring back to a simmer. Add the cream, reserving 2 to 3 tablespoons for the garnish, and stir to combine. Season with salt and freshly ground black pepper to taste.

Place the remaining heavy cream in a small mixing bowl and whisk vigorously for 1 minute or until slightly thickened and frothy. Ladle the hot soup into bowls, and drizzle over some of the whipped cream.

Garnish with chives and serve immediately.

split pea with ham

This split pea recipe gets its deep, rustic flavor from smoked pork hocks. A little fresh ground black pepper is the only garnish you'll need.

serves 6-8

2 tablespoons butter

1 onion, diced

2 ribs celery, diced

3 cloves minced garlic

Salt

2 smoked pork hocks

1 bay leaf

1 pound dried split peas, rinsed, drained

1 quart chicken broth

3 cups water

8 ounces (1½ cups) diced ham (optional)

Freshly ground black pepper to taste

Melt the butter in a soup pot over medium heat. Add the onion, celery, garlic, and pinch of salt. Cook, stirring, for about 3 minutes. Add the pork hocks, bay leaf, chicken broth, and water. Bring to a simmer, cover, turn heat to low, and cook for 1½ hours.

Add the split peas, cover and continue to cook on low, stirring occasionally for another 1 to 1½ hours, or until the peas are tender, and the soup has thickened. Additional water or broth can be added if the soup becomes too thick for your liking.

Remove the pork hocks, and when cool enough to handle, slice off any meat and add back to the soup (optional). Season with salt and fresh ground black pepper to taste, and serve hot with crackers.

new england clam chowder

America's most famous soup features one of the great flavor combinations of all time: bacon, clams and potatoes. This traditional recipe is much lighter in texture than the super-thick modern versions you may be used to.

serves 6

1 cup water

1 pound little neck clams, washed

2 slices bacon, cut into ¼ inch pieces

1 tablespoon butter

½ yellow onion, diced

2 tablespoons flour

2 (10 ounce) cans whole clams, drained

2 cups cold clam juice (Part of this may be made up from the drained canned clam liquid, but clam juice has a stronger clam flavor)

1½ pounds (5 medium) Idaho potatoes, peeled, and cut into ¼ inch cubes

1 cup milk

1 cup cream

Salt and freshly ground black pepper to taste

Fresh chopped parsley to garnish

Oyster crackers, to garnish

Bring one cup of water to a boil in a small saucepan over high heat. Add the little neck clams, cover tightly, and cook for a couple minutes, until the clams open. Remove the clams to a bowl and reserve. Strain the cooking liquid and reserve.

In large saucepan, over medium heat, cook the bacon in the butter until almost crisp. Remove the bacon with slotted spoon and reserve, leaving the butter and rendered bacon fat in the pan.

Reduce the heat to medium-low, and add the onions. Sauté until soft and translucent, about 5 minutes. Add the flour and cook, stirring, for 2 minutes. Whisk in the cold clam juice, slowly at first. Add the reserved clam cooking liquid. Bring back to a simmer and add the potatoes. Cover and cook for 20 minutes, or until the potatoes are tender.

Note: At this point some chowder-heads like to smash some of the potatoes against the bottom of the pan with a masher to add body to the soup. Optional!

Stir in the canned clams, milk, and cream. Reduce heat to low, and cook until just heated through. Do not boil. Add the reserved little neck clams, and cook for another minute. Taste and season with salt and freshly ground black pepper as needed.

Serve hot topped with the reserved bacon, parsley, and oyster crackers.

cream of mushroom soup

The secret to this delicious soup is patience. The longer you cook and caramelize the mushrooms in the butter, the deeper and "meatier" the flavor will be. Take your time, enjoy the aromas, and you'll be richly rewarded.

serves 4

¼ cup (½ stick) unsalted butter

2 pounds white button mushrooms, sliced (6 cups sliced mushrooms)

Salt

1 yellow onion, diced

1 tablespoon flour

4 cups chicken broth or stock

1 cup water

6 sprigs fresh thyme, tied into a bundle with kitchen string, plus some picked leaves to garnish

3 cloves garlic, peeled, left whole

1 cup heavy cream

Freshly ground black pepper

Melt the butter in a large heavy-bottomed soup pot over medium heat. Add the mushrooms and a big pinch of salt. Cook, stirring often, for 20 to 30 minutes, or until the mushrooms are golden brown. At first, the mushrooms will give up lots of water and simply boil, but as the liquid evaporates, they will start to brown and caramelize.

Note: At this point, you can reserve some of the browned mushrooms to garnish the soup later.

Once the mushrooms are beautifully browned, add the onions and cook over medium-low heat for about 5 more minutes. Add 1 tablespoon of flour and cook, stirring, for 1 minute. Whisk in the chicken broth and water. Add the thyme and garlic, and bring to a simmer. Reduce the heat to low, cover, and simmer gently for 1 hour.

Turn off heat, uncover, and allow the soup to cool for 15 minutes. Carefully puree the soup (in small batches!) in a blender until very smooth.

Pour soup back into the pot, and stir in the cream. (More broth or water can be added to adjust the thickness, if desired). Bring back to a simmer, and season with salt and freshly ground black pepper to taste.

Serve hot, topped with the reserved mushrooms and thyme leaves.

cream of broccoli soup with cheddar crouton

The cheesy cheddar croutons only make this nutritious broccoli soup more delicious.

serves 6

2 tablespoons unsalted butter

1 onion, diced

Salt

2 clove garlic, minced

2½ pounds broccoli crowns

4 cups (1 quart) chicken or vegetable broth

2 cups water

½ cup cream, optional

Freshly ground black pepper to taste

6 slices baguette or other bread

½ cup shredded sharp cheddar cheese

In a heavy soup pot, melt the butter over medium heat; when it begins to foam add the onion and a large pinch of salt. Cook, stirring occasionally, until the onions are soft and translucent, about 10 minutes. Add the garlic and cook for another minute.

While the onions are cooking, cut the tops (florettes) off the broccoli, and set aside. Cut the stems into ¼ inch slices, add to the tops and reserve. When the onions are ready, add the broth, water, and broccoli. Bring to a simmer, and cook until the broccoli is fork-tender.

While the soup is cooking, toast the bread and place on a foil-covered sheet pan. Top with the cheese; be sure to cover entire surface so the bread doesn't burn. Place under a broiler until the cheese is melted and bubbling.

When the broccoli is ready, remove from heat and puree using a stick blender, or carefully process the soup (in small batches!) in a blender until very smooth.

Pour the soup back into the pot. Add the cream, if using, and cook on medium-low until heated through. Season with salt and fresh ground black pepper to taste.

Ladle the broccoli soup into bowls and top with cheese croutons.

corn and clam chowder

This recipe is the perfect solution to the problem of not being able to decide between corn and clam chowder – hey, make both!

serves 4

1 pound 10 ounces fresh clams, or 10 ounces canned clams

2 tablespoons dry white wine (if using fresh clams)

4 teaspoons (½ stick) butter

1 large onion, finely chopped

1 small carrot, finely diced

3 tablespoons all-purpose flour

1¼ cups fish stock

¾ cup water (if using canned clams)

1 pound (3 medium) potatoes, diced

1 cup corn, thawed if frozen

2 cups whole milk

Salt and pepper

Chopped fresh parsley, to garnish

If using fresh clams, wash under cold running water. Discard any with broken shells or any that refuse to close when tapped. Put the clams into a heavy-bottom saucepan with the wine. Cover tightly, set over medium-high heat, and cook for 2 to 4 minutes, or until they open, shaking the pan occasionally. Discard any that remain closed. Remove the clams from the shells and strain the cooking liquid through a very fine mesh sieve; reserve both. If using canned clams, drain and rinse well.

Melt the butter in a large saucepan over medium-low heat. Add the onion and carrot and cook for 3 to 4 minutes, stirring frequently, until the onion is softened. Stir in the flour and continue cooking for 2 minutes.

Slowly add about half the stock and stir well, scraping the bottom of the pan to mix in the flour. Pour in the remaining stock and the reserved clam cooking liquid, or the water if using canned clams, and bring just to a boil, stirring.

Add the potatoes, corn, and milk and stir to combine. Reduce the heat and simmer gently, partially covered, for about 20 minutes, stirring occasionally, until all the vegetables are tender.

Chop the clams, if large. Stir in the clams and continue cooking for about 5 minutes until heated through. Taste and adjust the seasoning, if needed. Ladle the soup into bowls and sprinkle with parsley.

lobster bisque

A freshly steamed lobster is a wonderful thing, but to taste the true essence of lobster, bisque is the way to go.

serves 4

One (1-pound) lobster, steamed and split

3 tablespoons butter

1 small carrot, grated

1 celery stalk, finely chopped

1 leek, finely chopped

1 small onion, finely chopped

2 shallots, finely chopped

3 tablespoons brandy or Cognac

¼ cup dry white wine

5 cups water

1 tablespoon tomato paste

½ cup heavy cream, or to taste

6 tablespoons all-purpose flour

2 to 3 tablespoons water

Salt and pepper

Snipped fresh chives, to garnish

To prepare the lobster: Reserve the tomalley and roe (if any) together, covered and refrigerated. Remove the meat and cut into bite-sized pieces; cover and refrigerate. Chop the shell into large pieces.

Melt half the butter in a large saucepan over medium heat and add the lobster shell pieces. Cook until brown bits begin to stick on the bottom of the pan. Add the carrot, celery, leek, onion, and shallots. Cook, stirring, for 1½ to 2 minutes. Add the brandy and wine and bubble for 1 minute. Add the water, the tomato paste, and a pinch of salt, and bring to a boil. Reduce the heat, simmer for 30 minutes, and strain the stock, discarding the solids.

Melt the remaining butter in a small saucepan and add the tomalley and roe, if any. Add the cream, whisk to mix well, remove from the heat, and set aside.

Put the flour in a small mixing bowl and whisk in the cold water. Stir in a little of the hot stock mixture to make a smooth liquid. Bring the remaining lobster stock to a boil and whisk in the flour mixture. Boil gently for 4 to 5 minutes until the soup thickens, stirring frequently. Press the tomalley, roe, and cream mixture through a sieve into the soup. Reduce the heat and add the reserved lobster meat. Simmer gently until heated through. Add salt and pepper to taste, sprinkle with chives, and serve.

san francisco cioppino

There are two ways to make Cioppino – the way you do it, and the wrong way. This spicy fish stew just begs to be adapted to your personal tastes. Whether you make yours thick, thin, spicy or mild, just be sure to have lots of crusty sourdough bread around to soak up the sauce!

serves 4-6

2 tablespoons olive oil

2 tablespoons butter

1 rib celery, finely diced

1 onion, diced

Salt

6 cloves garlic, minced

2 cups good white wine

1 bay leaf

½ teaspoon dried oregano

½ teaspoon dried basil

½ teaspoon red pepper flakes,
or to taste

½ teaspoon Worcestershire sauce

1 can (28-ounce) tomato puree, or whole plum tomatoes, crushed fine

3 cups clam juice, fish stock, or water, plus more as needed to adjust thickness

1 teaspoon salt, or to taste

5 to 6 thin slices of lemon

1 cooked Dungeness crab (about 2 pounds), cracked and cleaned, or 1 pound frozen crabmeat, thawed

12 ounces fresh cod, or any other white fish, cut into 1-inch pieces

1 pound raw shrimp, peeled and deveined

1 pound fresh mussels, scrubbed

¼ cup chopped Italian parsley

Add the butter and olive oil to a large pot, and place on the stove over a medium-low heat. Add the celery and onions with a pinch of salt, and sauté them until soft, about 7 minutes. Add the garlic and sauté for one minute. Add the wine, turn the heat up to high, and bring to a boil.

Add the bay leaf, oregano, basil, pepper flakes, Worcestershire, tomato puree and clam juice. When the mixture comes back to a boil, reduce the heat to low and simmer uncovered for 45 minutes. Add water if the sauce gets too thick.

Turn the heat to high, and when the sauce returns to a rapid boil, add the remaining ingredients, stir, cover tightly, and cook for 5 minutes, or until the mussels open. Turn off the heat, taste for salt and spiciness, and adjust if needed.

Ladle Cioppino into large bowls and serve with lots of sourdough bread to soak up the sauce. Bonus points if you find some Anchor Steam beer and enjoy Cioppino like a real San Franciscan.

delicious chilis and stews

hearty beef stew

Not only is this classic stew delicious, it's also a frugal dish, since it uses relatively inexpensive chuck roast. Be sure to brown the beef very well to achieve a deep, rich flavor.

serves 6

3 pounds boneless chuck roast, cut into 2-inch pieces

2 tablespoons vegetable oil

1 teaspoon salt, plus more as needed

Freshly ground black pepper

2 yellow onions, cut into 1-inch pieces

3 tablespoons flour

3 cloves garlic, minced

4 cups cold beef stock or broth

3 carrots, peeled, cut into 1-inch pieces

2 stalks celery, cut into 1-inch pieces

1 tablespoon ketchup

1 bay leaf

¼ teaspoon dried rosemary

¼ teaspoon dried thyme

2 pounds (6 medium) Yukon gold potatoes, peeled, cut into large chunks

Fresh parsley to garnish, optional

Season the beef very generously with salt and freshly ground black pepper. Add vegetable oil to a large heavy pot or Dutch oven (one that has a tight fitting lid), and set over high heat. When the oil begins to smoke slightly, add the beef and brown very well. Work in batches if necessary. Once well-browned, remove the beef to a bowl with a slotted spoon, leaving the oil and beef drippings in the pot.

Lower the heat to medium, and add the onions to the pot; sauté about 5 minutes, or until translucent. Add the flour and cook for 2 minutes, stirring often. Add the garlic and cook for 1 minute. Whisk in 1 cup of the beef stock to deglaze the bottom of the pot, scraping up any browned bits caramelized on the bottom. Add the rest of the broth, carrots, celery, ketchup, bay leaf, thyme, rosemary, beef, and 1 teaspoon of salt.

Bring back to a gentle simmer, cover, and cook on low for 1 hour. Add potatoes, and simmer covered for another 30 minutes. Remove the cover, turn up the heat to medium, and cook, stirring occasionally, for another 30 minutes, or until the meat and vegetables are tender.

This last 30 minutes uncovered is not only to finish the cooking, but also to reduce and thicken the sauce. If the stew gets too thick, adjust with some more stock or water. Turn off heat, taste and adjust seasoning, and let sit for 15 minutes before serving. Garnish with fresh parsley, if desired.

"chili verde" green pork stew

Tomatillo-based green salsas are readily available in today's supermarkets, and make a great base for this flavorful, spicy pork stew.

serves 3

4 pounds boneless pork shoulder, cut into 2-inch cubes

Salt and pepper to taste

2 tablespoons vegetable oil

1 yellow onion, chopped

2 Anaheim chilies, seeded, diced

4 cups (two 16-ounce jars) green salsa (look for one with tomatillos as the main ingredient)

2 teaspoons ground cumin

1 teaspoon dried oregano

1 teaspoon sugar

½ teaspoon chipotle pepper

Sour cream and chopped cilantro to garnish, optional

Season the pork cubes with salt and pepper. In a heavy Dutch oven, heat the oil on medium-high, and sear the pork in batches until very well browned. Reserve the cooked pork in a bowl. Reduce the heat to medium and add the onions. Sauté until golden, about 5 minutes.

Add the rest of the ingredients, bring to a boil, reduce heat to low, cover, and simmer gently for 1½ to 2 hours, stirring occasionally, or until the pork is very tender. Taste and adjust seasoning.

Serve in bowls topped with sour cream and cilantro, if desired.

texas lone star chili

Sometimes simply called a "bowl of red", Texas-style chili has two major differences with regular chili; it uses cubed beef instead of ground, and it doesn't contain beans. Other than that, like home-style recipes, anything goes!

serves 6

2 tablespoons vegetable oil

3 pounds boneless beef chuck, cut in ½-inch cubes

2 green poblano chilies, seeded, diced

2 red Fresno chilies, seeded, minced

1 large onion, diced

3 cloves garlic, minced

2 tablespoons ancho chili powder, or to taste

1 Tbsp ground cumin

1 Tsp dried oregano

1½ Tsp salt

½ Tsp ground black pepper

¼ Tsp chipotle pepper

¼ Tsp cayenne pepper

3 cups beef broth

1 can (10-ounce) diced tomatoes with green chilies

1 Tbsp corn meal

Water as needed

¼ cup diced white onion and fresh chopped cilantro, optional

In a Dutch oven or cast iron pot, sear the beef in the oil over high heat, until well-browned. Do in batches if necessary. Add onions to the pot and sauté on medium heat for 5 minutes. Add the garlic and cook for one minute.

Add all remaining ingredients, except the corn meal, and bring to a boil, reduce the heat to low, cover, and simmer 1 hour, stirring occasionally. Uncover and stir in the corn meal. Continue cooking uncovered, stirring occasionally, for another hour, or until the meat is very tender. Water can be added any time during the cooking to adjust thickness. Be sure to occasionally skim off any fat that floats to the surface.

Taste for seasoning, and adjust if necessary. Serve hot garnished with white onions, cilantro, and/or any of your favorite chili fixings.

jambalaya

This Louisiana classic is truly one of our countries greatest culinary achievements. Spicy Creole jambalaya is rustic and refined all at the same time, and is legendary for its big flavored, crowd-pleasing abilities.

serves 3

1 Tbsp vegetable oil

1½ pounds spicy sausage, cut in ½-inch cubes

1 pound skinless, boneless chicken thighs, cut into 1-inch pieces

1 large yellow onion, diced

1 cup diced celery

1 cup diced green bell pepper

2 Tsp Cajun seasoning

1 Tsp dried thyme

1 Tsp salt

¼ Tsp freshly ground black pepper

¼ Tsp ground cayenne pepper,

2 cups uncooked long-grain rice

1 (14.5 ounce) can diced tomatoes

4 cups chicken broth

1 bay leaf

1 pound shrimp, peeled, deveined

½ bunch scallions, thinly sliced

Louisiana hot sauce

Heat the vegetable oil in a large Dutch oven, or other heavy pot, over medium-high heat. Add the sausage to the pan, and cook until lightly browned. Add the chicken, onion, celery, bell pepper, Cajun seasoning, salt, thyme, salt, black pepper, and cayenne. Cook for about 5 minutes, or until the onions begin to soften.

Turn up the heat to high. Add the tomatoes, broth, and bay leaf, and bring to a boil. Add the rice, and stir until completely combined. Cover, reduce heat to low, and simmer for 18 minutes. Stir in shrimp and scallions, cover, and cook 3 to 5 minutes, or until the rice is as tender as you like. Serve with hot sauce.

Note: You can really adjust this so many different ways. If you want a thinner, soupier stew, add a couple extra cups of broth. If you like your rice a bit firmer, cut the cooking time a few minutes. If you like it soft, give it a couple more minutes. You can use any types of sausage, as well as things like bacon, ham, and pork shoulder. This is a fun dish to experiment with. No two Jambalayas should be alike.

firehouse chili con carne

Is this called firehouse chili because it's the kind of hearty dish firemen love, or because of its spicy seasoning? Trick question; it's both!

serves 6

1 tablespoon vegetable oil

1 large yellow onion, diced

2½ pounds lean ground beef

3 cloves garlic, minced

¼ cup chile powder

1 tablespoon ground cumin

1 teaspoon freshly ground black pepper

½ teaspoon chipotle pepper

¼ teaspoon cayenne pepper

1 teaspoon dried oregano

1 teaspoon sugar

1 large green bell pepper, seeded and diced

1 large red bell pepper, seeded and diced

1 (15-ounce) can tomato sauce

2 tablespoons tomato paste

3 cups water, or more as needed

1 (15-ounce) can pinto beans, drained, not rinsed

1 (15-ounce) can kidney beans, drained, not rinsed

Add the vegetable oil and onions to a Dutch oven or other heavy pot. Place over medium-high heat and sauté for about 5 minutes, or until the onions begin to soften. Add the ground beef, and cook for about 10 minutes. As the beef browns, use a wooden spoon to break the meat into very small pieces.

Add the garlic, chili powder, ground cumin, black pepper, chipotle pepper, cayenne pepper, oregano, and sugar. Cook, stirring, for 2 minutes.

Stir in the bell peppers, tomato sauce, tomato paste, and water. Bring up to a simmer; reduce the heat to medium-low and cook, uncovered, stirring occasionally for 60 minutes.

After 60 minutes, stir in the beans and simmer for another 30 minutes. If needed, add more water anytime during the cooking to adjust desired thickness. Taste for salt and pepper, and adjust. Serve hot, garnished with sour cream, grated pepper jack, and fresh cilantro leaves, as desired.

chicken and white bean chili

When you're in the mood for the big, bold flavors of chili, but want something a little lighter, give this version a try.

serves 6

2 tablespoons vegetable oil

2 pounds boneless, skinless chicken thigh, cut into 1-inch pieces

1 onion, diced

3 cloves garlic, minced

1 teaspoon salt

2 tablespoons ground cumin

½ teaspoon ground chipotle pepper

¼ teaspoon cinnamon

½ teaspoon freshly ground black pepper

1 red bell pepper, seeded, diced

1 green bell pepper, seeded, diced

1 jalapeño pepper, seeded, diced

1 can (10-ounce) diced tomato with green chilies

3 cups chicken broth, more as needed

2 (15-ounce) cans white kidney beans, great northern, or navy beans, drained

Cayenne pepper

Chopped fresh cilantro to garnish, optional

Add oil to a large, heavy pot over medium-high heat. When the oil's hot, add the chunks of chicken, and sauté for 5 minutes. Add the onions, garlic, and salt; cook, stirring, for another 2 minutes. Add the cumin, chipotle, cinnamon, salt, and fresh ground black pepper; cook, stirring, for another minute.

Add the red bell pepper, green bell pepper, jalapeño pepper, diced tomato with green chilies, and chicken broth. Bring to a simmer, turn heat to low, and cook, stirring occasionally, for 30 minutes.

Stir in the beans and simmer another 30 minutes. Taste and adjust for salt and pepper. Serve hot with a shake of cayenne pepper, and cilantro, if desired.

chicken and sausage gumbo

This hearty Cajun/Creole stew's name is derived from the African word for okra. This signature ingredient not only gives the gumbo a great flavor, but also thickens the dish. The other key element is the "roux," which is a slowly browned mixture of flour and oil. The darker you cook the roux, the stronger the flavor.

serves 6

1/3 **cup vegetable oil**

1/3 **cup flour**

1 onion, diced

3 ribs celery, diced

2 green bell pepper, seeded, diced

½ **cup minced green onions**

3 cloves garlic, crushed

1 pound of spicy smoked sausage, cut in 1 inch pieces

6 cups chicken broth

1 can (10-ounce) diced tomatoes with green chilies

1½ **pounds boneless, skinless chicken thighs, cut in 2-inch pieces**

1 Tbsp Cajun seasoning

1 Tsp salt

¼ **Tsp cayenne pepper, or to taste**

½ **Tsp black pepper**

2 cups frozen cut okra, thawed, drained

1 pound shrimp, peeled, deveined

To make the roux: In a heavy Dutch oven or pot, cook the oil and flour over medium low heat, stirring with a wooden spoon, until it's a light, nutty brown color.

Add the onion, celery, and bell pepper to the roux and cook for another 5 minutes to soften the vegetables. Add the green onions, garlic, and sausage; stir, and cook for 3 minutes.

Add the broth, tomatoes, chicken, Cajun seasoning, salt, cayenne pepper, and black pepper. Bring to a boil, reduce to low, and simmer, stirring occasionally, for 1 hour. Stir in the okra and simmer for another 30 minutes, or until the chicken is very tender.

Stir in the shrimp and cook for 3 to 4 minutes, or until they're cooked through. Taste for salt and spice, and adjust seasoning if needed. Serve hot with cooked long-grain rice.

hearty meals

king ranch chicken casserole

The flavors in this easy chicken casserole are as big as Texas, the state where this hearty dish was born.

serves 6-8

1 cup of chicken broth

1 can cream of mushroom soup

1 can cream of chicken soup

1 (10-ounce) can diced tomatoes with green chilies

2 tablespoons sour cream

1 white onion, diced small

1 red bell pepper, diced

1 green bell pepper, diced

2 jalapeño, seeded, diced fine, optional

2 teaspoons ancho chile powder

2 teaspoons cumin

1½ teaspoons salt

½ teaspoon dried oregano

½ teaspoon chipotle chile powder, or to taste

One (4 to 5-pound) cooked chicken, roughly shredded

8 ounces (1 cup) grated sharp cheddar cheese

8 to 10 corn tortillas, quartered

Preheat oven to 350°F. Combine the chicken broth, soups, tomatoes, sour cream, onions, peppers, and spices in a mixing bowl and stir to combine thoroughly. Once mixed, spoon ½ cup of the sauce into a separate bowl and reserve for the top of the casserole.

Place half the chicken in a lightly oiled 9 x 13-inch casserole dish. Spoon over half the sauce mixture, and spread evenly. Top with a third of the cheese. Top with half the tortillas. There is no need to overlap the tortilla pieces; a single layer is fine.

Top with the rest of the chicken, and then spread over the rest of the sauce. Top with the next third of the cheese, then the rest of the tortillas to cover the surface completely. Use a spatula to spread over the ½ cup of reserved sauce. Top with the last third of the cheese.

Bake uncovered for 40 minutes, or until golden brown and bubbly. Let rest for 15 minutes before serving.

braised lamb shanks

Only make this lamb shanks recipe if you really enjoy flavorful, succulent, fork-tender meat.

serves 6

6 lamb shanks, about 5½ pounds

2 tablespoons olive oil

½ teaspoon dried rosemary

½ teaspoon dried thyme

Salt and freshly ground black pepper

1 tablespoon butter

1 onion, diced

1 rib celery, diced

1 large carrot, diced

1 tablespoon flour

4 cloves garlic, minced

½ cup red wine

1 cup chicken broth

1 tablespoon balsamic vinegar

½ cup water

⅛ teaspoon cinnamon

1 teaspoon minced fresh rosemary leaves

Preheat oven to 450°F. Place the shanks in a deep, 15 x 10-inch roasting pan, large enough to fit the shanks in one layer. Rub with the olive oil, rosemary and thyme; season with salt and pepper. Roast for 30 minutes to brown.

While the lamb is browning, place a saucepan on medium-high heat, and add the butter. When the butter foams, add the onion, celery, and carrot. Cook for 6 to 7 minutes, until the vegetables soften and the edges start to brown.

Stir in the flour and cook for 1 minute. Add the garlic and cook for 1 minute more. Stir in the wine. When the wine comes to a boil, stir in the broth, balsamic vinegar, water, and cinnamon. Return to a boil, turn off and reserve.

When the lamb has finished browning, remove, and turn the oven down to 325°F. Pour the sauce over the meat. Cover with foil, crimping the edges to form a tight seal. Roast for 1 hour, lift the foil, turn over the shanks, rewrap and cook for 1 more hour, or until fork tender. Remove the lamb shanks to a large bowl, and cover with foil to keep warm.

Pour the braising liquid into a saucepan, and boil on high heat for 10 minutes, or until reduced by half and has thickened slightly. Skim off any excess fat. Add the fresh rosemary, taste and adjust the seasoning. Transfer the lamb shanks to a serving platter, and serve topped with the sauce.

sloppy joes

The secret to a great Sloppy Joe sandwich is slowly simmering the beefy mixture down until it's rich and tender. By the way, you should always serve Sloppy Joes with a fork, but you should never need to use it.

serves 4-6

1½ pounds lean ground beef

½ onion, diced

2 cloves garlic, minced

1 green bell pepper, seeded and diced

2 cups water, divided

¾ cup ketchup

1½ tablespoons firmly packed brown sugar

1 teaspoon Dijon mustard

Dash of Worcestershire sauce

1½ teaspoons salt, or to taste

½ teaspoon ground black pepper

Cayenne pepper to taste

Hamburger buns, or other soft rolls

Place the ground beef and onions into a cold, large skillet and put over medium heat. Cook, stirring, until the beef begins to brown. As it cooks, break the meat into very small pieces with a spatula. The smaller the better.

Add the garlic and green pepper; cook stirring for 2 minutes. Add 1 cup of water. Bring to a simmer, scraping the bottom of the pan with a spatula to dissolve any browned bits.

Stir in the ketchup, brown sugar, mustard, Worcestershire Sauce, salt, pepper, and the last cup of water. Bring to a simmer, reduce heat to low, and simmer for 30 to 45 minutes, or until most of the liquid has been evaporated, and the meat mixture is thick, rich, and tender. Taste and adjust the seasoning. Serve hot on soft rolls.

barbecued baby back ribs

It would be great if we all had a big ol' smoker in the backyard to make authentic barbecue with, but when done right, the oven does a surprisingly excellent job turning out tender, tasty ribs.

serves 6

2 full racks baby back pork ribs, trimmed of excess fat, patted dry

For the rub

1/3 cup packed light brown sugar

3 tbsps kosher salt

1 tsp ground black pepper

1 tbsp smoked or regular paprika

½ tsp ground chipotle pepper

½ tsp dried thyme

½ tsp dried mustard

½ tsp garlic powder

½ tsp onion powder

¼ tsp cayenne pepper

1½ cups Kansas City style barbecue sauce

Combine the spice rub ingredients in a small bowl and mix thoroughly. Place each rack of ribs in the center of its own large piece of heavy-duty aluminum foil. Generously apply the dry rub to each side of the two racks (more so on the meat side). Wrap each rack in foil; transfer to the refrigerator for at least 4 hours – overnight is even better.

Pre-heat oven to 250°F.

Place the two foil-wrapped racks on a baking sheet and place in oven. Bake for 2 hours. Remove the ribs from oven, and using tongs, carefully open the foil (excess fat can be poured off). Place both racks on one piece of the foil, and brush barbecue sauce generously on both sides

Increase the oven temperature to 350°F.

Return pan of ribs to the oven. Continue cooking, brushing on more barbecue sauce several times, until the ribs are fork tender and well glazed, about 30 to 45 minutes.

Remove and let rest for 5 minutes before cutting and serving. Ribs can be tossed in additional sauce if desired, and/or served with extra sauce on the side.

yankee pot roast

This recipe uses a "7-bone" chuck roast (named for the numerical shape of the bone), which is a tough, but a super-flavorful cut of beef that becomes beautifully fork-tender after a long, slow braise.

serves 3

One 5-pound "7-bone" beef chuck roast, or any large chuck roast

Salt and freshly ground black pepper to taste

2 tablespoons vegetable oil

1 tablespoon butter

1 onion, diced

2 ribs celery, chopped

2 tablespoons flour

3 cloves garlic, minced

½ cup red wine

2 teaspoons tomato paste

2 cups chicken broth

1 bay leaf

1 teaspoon dried thyme

½ teaspoon salt

1½ pounds (10-12) new potatoes

4 carrots, peeled, cut in large chunks

1 pound parsnips, peeled, cut in large chunks

1 tablespoon melted butter

2 tablespoons fresh chopped parsley

Preheat oven to 425°F. Season the beef with salt and pepper. Place a Dutch oven on a high heat on the stove, add the vegetable oil. When the oil is hot, brown the beef, about 5 minutes per side. Remove the meat to a platter, and turn the heat down to medium.

Add the butter, onions, celery, and a pinch of salt. Sauté for 4 to 5 minutes, then add the flour. Cook, stirring, 2 minutes; add the garlic, cook for 1 minute. Whisk in the wine, scraping to deglaze the browned bits from the bottom of the pot. Add the tomato paste, bring to boil, and pour in the chicken broth.

Add the bay leaf, thyme, and salt. Bring the liquid to a simmer, and place the beef back into the pot. Turn the heat to low, and simmer gently for about 45 minutes per pound, or until fork tender. After 2 hours, carefully turn the beef over.

To prepare the vegetables: Add the potatoes, carrots, and parsnips to a shallow roasting pan. Drizzle fat from the beef's braising liquid over the vegetables, along with the melted butter. Toss the vegetables to coat, and season with salt and pepper. Roast in the oven for 20 minutes. Remove and reserve.

About 30 minutes before the beef is done, add the vegetables to the pot. Continue cooking until the beef and vegetables are tender. Taste and adjust for salt and pepper. Remove the beef to a platter. Cut into thick slices or simply tear into large chucks, and serve with the vegetables and gravy. Top with fresh parsley.

old-fashioned chicken and dumplings

This is one of the ultimate comfort foods. Some folks like their dumplings light and airy, while others prefer them more hearty and dense. These are somewhere in between, but every bit as delicious.

serves 6

2 tablespoons vegetable oil

(4 to 5-pound) One chicken, cut in quarters, backbone reserved

1 quart chicken broth

3 cups water

4 cloves garlic, peeled

1 bay leaf

4 springs fresh thyme

5 tablespoons butter

2 carrots, chopped

2 ribs celery, chopped

1 large onion, chopped

5 tablespoons flour

1½ teaspoon salt

Freshly ground black pepper

Dash of hot sauce

For the dumplings

1¾ cups all-purpose flour

1 teaspoon salt

2 teaspoons baking powder

¼ teaspoon baking soda

3 tablespoons cold butter

2 tablespoons chopped scallions

¼ cup buttermilk

¾ cup milk

Heat the oil in a Dutch oven on the stove over high heat. Brown the chicken pieces and add broth, water, garlic, bay leaf and thyme. Boil and then turn heat down and simmer covered for 30 minutes, then, remove chicken to a bowl. Strain the cooking liquid into a separate bowl, skimming off any fat.

Place the Dutch oven over medium heat and add butter, carrots, celery and onion. Sauté for 5 minutes before stirring in the flour. Cook for 2 minutes and then whisk in the reserved cooking liquid one cup at a time. Add salt, pepper, and hot sauce. Reduce the heat and simmer covered for 30 minutes until the vegetables are tender.

Remove the chicken meat from the bones and tear into chunks. Stir the chicken pieces into the cooked vegetables. Cover and reduce heat to lowest possible temperature.

To make the dumplings: Combine flour, salt, baking powder and baking soda into a mixing bowl. Cut in the cold butter using a pastry blender until the mixture resembles coarse crumbs. Add the scallions, buttermilk, and milk and stir with a fork into a thick dough. Turn the heat under the Dutch oven to medium and drop large balls of the dumpling dough into the mixture. Cover and cook for 15 minutes until the dumplings are firm and cooked in the middle.

"london broil" with brown gravy

London broil is not a cut of beef, but instead a way to prepare it.
London broil is usually made with a thick top round steak, but can
also be done with flank or sirloin steak. By the way, leftover London
broil makes fantastic cold roast beef sandwiches.

serves 4-6

¼ cup balsamic vinegar

2 tbsps olive oil

4 cloves crushed garlic

½ tsp dried rosemary

2 lbs top round "London
Broil" steak,
about 2 inches thick

1 tbsp freshly ground black
pepper

Kosher salt as needed

1 bunch green onions,
washed

For the gravy

½ cup butter

½ yellow onion, diced

½ cup all-purpose flour

1 clove garlic, minced

1 quart cold beef broth
(as high-quality as
possible!)

2 tsps tomato paste

1 tsp Dijon mustard

1 tsp Worcestershire sauce

Salt and black pepper to
taste

In a small bowl whisk together the vinegar, oil, garlic, and
rosemary. Place the beef on a plate and poke both sides all
over with a fork. Transfer to plastic freezer bag and pour in
the marinade. Refrigerate overnight.

Turn broiler on high. Make a bed of green onions on an
oven-safe pan. Remove the London broil from the marinade
and pat dry. Brush both sides lightly with vegetable oil. Salt
and pepper generously on both sides. Place on the pan, over
the onions. Broil about 6 inches under the flame for
approximately 7 to 8 minutes per side for medium rare, or to
an internal temperature of 130°F.

Transfer to plate, cover with foil and let rest for 10 minutes.
Serve topped with hot beef gravy

For the gravy: In a saucepan, melt the butter. Add the
onions, cooking until golden brown. Add the flour and cook,
stirring until the mixture is golden-brown. Add the garlic and
slowly whisk in the beef broth. Add the rest of the
ingredients. Bring to a slow boil and then reduce the heat to
low and simmer for 25 minutes.

roast pork tenderloin
with black cherry sauce

Not only is pork tenderloin very lean, it is one of the easiest cuts of meat to cook. A sweet, tangy cherry sauce pairs perfectly with the pork's spicy black pepper crust.

serves 6

2 trimmed pork tenderloins (about 1½ lbs each)

Kosher salt to taste

¼ cup coarsely ground black pepper

2 tbsps vegetable oil

1 clove garlic, crushed

⅓ cup balsamic vinegar

½ cup black cherry preserves

1 cup chicken stock

2 tbsps cold unsalted butter

Pre-heat oven to 375°F.

Coat all sides of the pork tenderloins generously with salt and black pepper, and to taste. Heat the vegetable oil, in a large, ovenproof frying pan, over medium-high heat, until it begins to smoke. Sear the pork on all sides, about 2 minutes per side. Turn off the heat; place the pan in the center of the preheated oven.

Roast the pork for about 25 minutes, or until the internal temperature reaches 140°F. for medium. When the pork is cooked, remove it from the pan to a plate and cover loosely with foil to rest while the sauce is made.

Pour off the excess fat from the frying pan, and place over high heat. Add the garlic and cook for just 15 seconds, then add the vinegar, cherry preserves, and chicken stock. Cook, scraping the bottom of the pan with a wooden spoon to deglaze the pan drippings.

Boil until the sauce reduces by about half, about 6 to 7 minutes. Turn off the heat, and whisk in the cold butter, stirring constantly until the butter disappears. Taste for salt, and adjust the seasoning. Slice the pork and serve with the sauce spooned over.

chicken and mushroom marsala over garlic toasts

Chicken Marsala usually calls for chicken to be pounded out thin and dredged in flour before cooking. This adaptation uses whole breasts for a moister, easier version. When buying the wine, be sure to get regular Marsala, not the sweet dessert style.

serves 4

4 thick slices Italian or French bread

Olive oil as needed

1 whole garlic clove

4 large boneless chicken breasts, skin on

Salt and freshly ground black pepper to taste

2 tablespoons olive oil

8 large white mushrooms, sliced

2 tablespoons finely minced shallots

2 cloves garlic, minced

1½ tablespoons flour

1½ cup Marsala wine

2 cups chicken broth

2 tablespoons cold butter, cut in small pieces

1 tablespoon freshly chopped parsley

Lightly brush the bread slices with olive oil, and toast under a broiler. Remove and rub the whole garlic clove over each slice. Set aside.

Season the chicken breasts with salt and pepper. Heat the olive oil in a large skillet over medium-high flame. Place the chicken skin-side down and sear for 5 minutes. Turn over and cook for another 5 minutes. Remove to a plate and reserve.

Add the mushrooms, and a pinch of salt to the skillet, reduce the heat to medium and cook the mushrooms until they soften and give up their juices. Continue cooking until the liquid evaporates and the mushrooms brown. Add the shallots and garlic; cook, stirring, 1 minute. Add the flour; cook, stirring, for 2 minutes.

Carefully add the Marsala, turn up the heat to high, and cook, stirring, for 2 minutes. Scrape the bottom of the pan with a whisk to deglaze caramelized bits. Add the chicken broth and boil until the sauce begins to thicken slightly.

Reduce the heat to very low, and return the chicken breasts to the skillet, tossing them in the sauce to coat and warming the chicken. Plate each chicken breast on top of a slice of toasted bread. Add the parsley, and butter to the sauce and whisk until butter disappears. Adjust seasoning with salt and pepper to taste. Spoon the sauce over the top and serve immediately.

maple-brined roast pork loin
with mustard glaze

Brining is a fantastic technique for a pork loin roast, since it keeps the lean meat very moist and flavorful. By the way, you can use this same brine recipe for a whole chicken, or turkey breast.

serves 4-6

For the brine

1 quart cold water

¼ cup salt

½ cup maple syrup

4 cloves garlic, crushed

1 tbsp cracked black pepper

2 tbsps chopped fresh rosemary leaves

3½ lbs boneless pork loin roast, trimmed

1 tbsp vegetable oil

Salt and freshly ground black pepper to taste

For the mustard crust

¹/₃ cup maple syrup

3 tbsps Dijon mustard, or to taste

2 tbsps plain breadcrumbs

1 tbsp melted butter

Pre-heat oven to 450°F.

Pour the water into a plastic container, one with a lid, large enough to fit the pork. Add the salt, maple syrup, garlic, black pepper, and rosemary. Whisk together until the salt is dissolved. Add the pork loin roast. The pork should be fully submerged, so place a small plate on if necessary. Cover tightly and refrigerate overnight, or up to 24 hours.

Remove the pork from the brine, and pat dry with paper towels. Rub with the oil, season with salt and fresh ground black pepper. Place fatter side down, in a small roasting pan. Roast in oven for 15 minutes. While it roasts, mix the maple syrup and mustard in a small bowl. In a separate small bowl mix the breadcrumbs with the melted butter.

Remove, and turn down the oven to 325°F. Turn the pork over, so the fatter side is up, and spread on enough of the maple mustard mixture to generously coat the top (the rest of this mixture can be served at the table). Sprinkle over the buttered breadcrumbs.

Return to the oven and roast for another 45 to 60 minutes, or until the internal temp reaches 155°F.

Let rest for at least 15 minutes before slicing and serving along with any leftover maple mustard.

hunter's chicken

Also commonly known as chicken cacciatore, this recipe's name is deliciously ironic. What kind of hunter is stalking and shooting chickens?

serves 4

2 tablespoons olive oil

8 large chicken thighs (about 3½ pounds)

Salt and freshly ground black pepper

1 large onion, sliced

8 ounces fresh mushrooms, thickly sliced

1 tablespoon flour

½ cup white wine

1½ cup chicken broth

1 cup chopped tomato

8 cloves garlic, peeled (left whole)

3 springs fresh rosemary

1 bay leaf

1 teaspoon dried oregano

½ teaspoon red pepper flakes,
or to taste

1 teaspoon salt

1 red bell pepper, seeded, sliced

1 green bell pepper, seeded, sliced

Preheat oven to 350°F. Season the chicken generously with salt and freshly ground black pepper. Place a heavy Dutch oven on the stove over a medium-high heat; add the olive oil and brown the chicken thighs well on all both sides. Remove the chicken, and add the onions and mushrooms. Reduce the heat to medium and sauté for about 5 minutes, until the onions soften.

Stir in the flour and cook for one minute. Stir in the wine, tomato, and chicken broth; bring to a boil, scraping the bottom with a wooden spoon to release the caramelized bits.

Add the garlic, rosemary, bay leaf, oregano, pepper flakes, and salt. Stir to combine. Place the chicken pieces, and any juices, over the sauce, and top with the sliced peppers. Cover with the lid and place in oven for 45 minutes. Remove the lid and roast for 15 minutes more.

Remove from oven and let rest, covered, for 10 minutes. Skim any excess fat from the top of the sauce. Taste and adjust seasoning. Serve over pasta, rice, or polenta.

prime rib of beef

A big, beautiful prime rib is the ideal special-occasion roast. This simple preparation shows off the lovely (and by lovely, I mean expensive) meat's best qualities—the deep, rich flavor, and juicy, buttery texture.

serves 2 portions per rib

1 standing prime rib of beef roast (4 to 7 ribs, about 9 to 18 pounds), trimmed and tied

Room temperature butter, about ½ tablespoon per rib bone

Fresh coarsely-ground black pepper

Kosher salt (or other larger grain, flake-style salt), as needed

2 tablespoons flour

4 cups cold beef broth, or veal stock if available

1 tablespoon fresh chopped tarragon, optional

For the sauce
6 tablespoons creamed horseradish sauce

6 tablespoons sour cream

Preheat oven to 450°F. Place the meat in a large, sturdy metal roasting pan. No rack is needed as bones form a natural rack. Rub the entire surface of the roast with butter, and season very generously with kosher salt and black pepper. Leave the meat out at room temperature for 2 hours.

When the oven is hot, put the roast in for 20 minutes to sear the outside. After 20 minutes turn the oven down to 325°F., and roast until the desired internal temperature is reached (see below). Some use 15 minutes per pound as a rule of thumb, but a good digital thermometer is more accurate.

The following are internal temperatures for removing the beef and not the final temperature. The meat will continue to cook after it's removed.

Rare: Remove at 110-115°F. (Final temp about 120-125°F.)

Medium-Rare: Remove at 120-125°F. (Final temp about 130-135°F.)

Medium: Remove at 130-135°F. (Final temp about 140-145°F.)

Transfer to a serving platter, and let the meat rest, loosely covered with foil, for at least 30 minutes.

For the sauce: In a small bowl combine the horseradish sauce and sour cream. Serve with the meat.

corned beef and cabbage

Corned beef and cabbage is the traditional St. Patrick's Day meal, but why enjoy this easy recipe only once a year?

serves 6-10

3½ to 5 pounds corned beef brisket

Spice packet from the corned beef package

2 teaspoons coarsely ground black pepper

1 bay leaf

Salt as needed

2 pounds (about 6) white potatoes, cut in quarters

4 carrots, peeled, cut in chunks

1 onions, diced

3 stalks celery, diced

1 small green cabbage, cored, cut in 8 wedges

Place the corned beef, 1 teaspoon of the salt, pepper, and spices into a large pot along with 3 quarts of cold water. Cover and bring to a boil over high heat. Turn down the heat to low and slowly simmer for 2¹/₂ hours.

Add the potatoes, carrots, onions, and celery. Simmer, covered for 20 minutes. Add the cabbage and cook covered for another 20 minutes, or until the potatoes and vegetables are tender. Remove the beef, and let rest 5 minutes. Slice against the grain and serve with the cabbage, potatoes, vegetables, and some of the cooking liquid. Serve with rye or dark bread and mustard on the side.

chicken pot pie

You can make this in a casserole dish and serve it family-style, but there's something special about individual chicken pot pies. With these you always have that perfect balance between the thick, chunky filling, and the crisp, buttery crust.

serves 6

1 tablespoon olive oil

8 ounces white button mushrooms, sliced

1 onion, diced

2 cups sliced carrots

1 cup sliced celery

4 cups cold chicken broth

6 tablespoons butter

½ cup all-purpose flour

2 pounds skinless, boneless chicken breasts, cut in 1-inch cubes

1 cup frozen green peas

1 teaspoon chopped fresh thyme leaves or a pinch of dried

1 teaspoon salt

¼ teaspoon black pepper

1½ pounds pie dough (enough for two 10-inch pies)

1 egg, beaten

Preheat oven to 400°F. In a large saucepan, sauté the mushrooms and onions in the olive oil over medium heat until golden. Add the carrots, celery, and 2 cups of chicken broth. Bring to a boil, reduce to low and simmer until the vegetables are almost tender.

Melt the butter in a large saucepan over medium heat. Whisk in the flour and cook, stirring, for 4 minutes, or until the flour is a light tan color and smells like cooked piecrust. Slowly whisk in 2 cups of cold chicken broth. Simmer over medium-low heat until the mixture thickens. Remove from heat, and reserve.

Add the vegetables and broth from the other pan when ready, and stir to combine. Add the chicken, peas, thyme, salt and pepper. Bring back to a simmer and cook, stirring, for 5 minutes. Taste for seasoning and set aside until needed.

Divide the pot pie filling among 6 large (15-ounce) ramekins (fill to ½ inch from the top). Cut out circles of pie dough 1 inch larger than the width of the ramekins. Place the dough over the pot pies. Go around each piece of dough, folding ½ inch over to form a rim. If desired, pinch with your finger tips to form a crimped edge. Cut a small "X" in the center of each crust.

Place the ramekins on a baking sheet. Brush the tops with the beaten egg. Bake for 35 to 40 minutes, or until pies are golden brown and bubbly. Cool for 15 minutes before serving.

classic tuna noodle casserole

It's a mystery why the creamy and comforting tuna noodle casserole became synonymous with bad home cooking. There's nothing not to like about this great American retro classic.

serves 6

3 tablespoons butter

½ yellow onion, finely diced

3 tablespoons flour

3½ cups cold milk

1 (10-ounce) can condensed cream of mushroom soup

1 teaspoon salt

¼ teaspoon freshly ground black pepper

12 ounce package dry egg noodles

2 (7 ounce) cans tuna, well drained, crumbled

¾ cup frozen peas, thawed, drained

1 cup shredded cheddar cheese

½ cup shredded Monterey jack cheese

½ cup plain bread crumbs

2 tablespoons olive oil

Preheat oven to 350°F. Melt the butter in a medium saucepan, over medium-low heat, and sauté the onions for about 4 minutes, or until translucent. Turn up the heat to medium; add the flour, and cook, stirring, for another 2 minutes. While whisking vigorously, slowly pour in one cup of the cold milk.

When the mixture begins to simmer, add the rest of the milk, can of mushroom soup, salt, and pepper. Cook, stirring occasionally, until the sauce thickens, and comes to a simmer. Remove from heat, and reserve.

Cook noodles in boiling salted water, one minute less than the directions call for. Drain well, and add to a large mixing bowl. Add the sauce, tuna, peas and about two-thirds of the cheese. Mix with a spatula to combine.

Pour the mixture into a lightly oiled 9x13-inch casserole dish, and top with the rest of the cheese. Mix the breadcrumbs and olive oil together in a small bowl until combined. Sprinkle evenly over the casserole. Bake for 35 minutes, or until browned and bubbly.

wild salmon cakes with tarragon aioli

Not only is canned salmon perfect for a recipe like this, but it is wild-caught, and nutritionally superior to fresh farmed salmon.

makes 6

1 (15-ounce) can red or pink salmon

¹/₃ cup plain breadcrumbs, plus more as needed

1 large egg, beaten

1 Tbsp mayonnaise

1 Tbsp capers, chopped

1 Tbsp fresh lemon juice

1 clove garlic, crushed, minced fine

1 Tsp fresh tarragon, chopped fine

½ Tsp Dijon mustard

½ Tsp salt

¼ Tsp black pepper

2 Tbsp olive oil

1 Tbsp butter

Fresh lemon wedges to garnish

For the sauce

½ teaspoon Dijon mustard

2 tablespoons mayonnaise

2 tablespoons sour cream

2 teaspoons fresh tarragon, chopped

1 teaspoon lemon juice

Pinch of cayenne pepper

Pinch of salt

To make the sauce: Combine all the sauce ingredients in a small bowl and whisk to combine. Refrigerate until needed.

Add the salmon to a mixing bowl, along with ¹/₃ cup breadcrumbs and the rest of the ingredients, except the oil and butter. Mix with a fork until thoroughly combined. Refrigerate for 30 minutes.

Shape into 6 patties about 1-inch thick, and place on a plate lightly dusted with breadcrumbs. Dust the tops of the salmon cakes lightly with breadcrumbs also. Heat the oil and butter in a large skillet over medium heat until the butter melts. Cook the salmon cakes for about 3 to 4 minutes per side, or until golden brown and heated through. Serve hot with the sauce and fresh lemon wedges.

on the side

macaroni and cheese

Did you know that Thomas Jefferson is credited with inventing macaroni and cheese? That has nothing to do with the recipe, but it's good to know in case you end up on one of those trivia game shows.

serves 6

6 tablespoons butter, divided

½ cup minced onion

3 tablespoons all-purpose flour

2¾ cups milk

½ teaspoon freshly chopped thyme leaves (or pinch of dry), optional

Pinch of nutmeg

Pinch of cayenne pepper

Salt and pepper

2 cups dry elbow macaroni

1 cup (½ pound) shredded cheddar cheese

½ cup (¼ pound) shredded Gruyère cheese, or other high-quality Swiss cheese

²/₃ cup breadcrumbs

Preheat oven to 350°F. Melt 4 tablespoons of the butter in a medium saucepan over medium heat. Sauté the onions in the butter for 4 to 5 minutes, until translucent. Do not brown. Stir in the flour, and cook for 2 minutes. Whisk in the cold milk, and cook, stirring, until the mixture comes to a simmer and thickens slightly. Turn off the heat and stir in the thyme, nutmeg, pinch of cayenne pepper, salt and pepper to taste. Set aside until needed.

Boil the elbow macaroni in salted water, one minute less than the package directions state. Drain well and add to a large mixing bowl. Add the white sauce, and the cheeses, and fold with a spatula until thoroughly combined.

Transfer into a lightly buttered 9x13-inch baking dish. Melt 2 tablespoons of butter and mix with the breadcrumbs. Scatter evenly over the top of the casserole. Bake for 40 to 45 minutes, or until bubbly and golden brown.

Note: Cover loosely with foil towards the end of the cooking, if the top is getting too brown for your liking.

boston baked beans

They don't call Boston "Beantown" for nothing. This great
Classic side dish has been spreading happiness at picnics
and potlucks for hundreds of years.

serves 10

1 pound dry navy beans

6 cups water

Pinch of baking soda

1 bay leaf

6 strips bacon, cut in
½-inch pieces (traditionally
salt pork is used, and if
desired 4 ounces can be
substituted for the bacon)

1 yellow onion, diced

⅓ cup molasses

¼ cup packed dark brown
sugar

1 teaspoon dry mustard

1½ teaspoon salt, or to
taste

½ teaspoon freshly ground
black pepper

Preheat oven to 300°F. Soak the beans in the water overnight
in a large saucepan. Add a pinch of baking soda and bay
leaf, and bring to a boil. Reduce the heat to medium and
simmer for 10 minutes. Drain into a colander set over a large
bowl, and reserve the liquid.

Transfer the drained beans into a small Dutch oven, or a
2 ½-quart bean pot, and add the rest of the ingredients. Stir
until combined. Add enough of the reserved water to just
barely cover the beans.

Cover the pot tightly and place in the oven for 1 hour.
Uncover and check the liquid level. Add more reserved liquid
if the beans are too dry. Cover and cook 1 more hour.
Uncover and test the beans; they should be starting to get
tender, but if they're still firm, cover and cook a bit longer,
adding a splash of water if they're getting too dry.

When just tender, turn the heat up to 350°F, and continue
to cook uncovered for another 30 minutes to reduce the
liquid and create a thick, syrupy sauce. Serve hot or at
room temperature.

Note: The cooking times will vary based on the size and
shape of the baking vessel, but the process will not. Simply
bake the beans covered until just tender, and finish
uncovered until the liquid has thickened slightly.

scalloped potatoes

For those times when regular potatoes just won't do. This creamy, cheesy scoop of side dish heaven looks great next to any meaty main course.

serves 8

2 tbsps butter, divided

1 tbsp all-purpose flour

1 cup cream

2 cups milk

1 tsp salt

Pinch of nutmeg

Pinch of white pepper

4 springs fresh thyme

2 cloves garlic minced

4½ lbs russet potatoes, sliced thin

Salt and freshly ground black pepper to taste

4 oz grated Swiss gruyere or white cheddar

Pre-heat oven to 375°F.

Use half the butter to grease a 15 x 10 inch baking dish.

Melt the rest of the butter in a saucepan over medium heat. Whisk in the flour, and cook, stirring constantly, for 2 minutes. Whisk in the cream and milk, and bring to a simmer. Add the salt, nutmeg, white pepper, thyme, and garlic. Reduce heat to low, and simmer for 5 minutes. Remove the thyme springs; reserve.

Layer half the potatoes in the baking dish. Season generously with salt and freshly ground black pepper. Top with half of the milk mixture. Top with half the cheese. Repeat with the remaining potatoes, sauce, and cheese.

Bake for about 1 hour, or until the top is browned and the potatoes are tender. Let rest for 15 minutes before serving.

garlic and herb steak fries

Unless you have a commercial deep fryer in your kitchen, regular French fries are probably best left to the neighborhood burger joint. On the contrary, these crusty and delicious, oven-roasted steak fries are easily made at home.

makes 8 portions

4 medium Idaho potatoes, scrubbed and rinsed

3 tablespoons olive oil

4 cloves garlic, minced and mashed against the cutting board with the flat of a knife

½ teaspoon dried rosemary, crushed fine

½ teaspoon dried oregano

½ teaspoon dried thyme

½ teaspoon paprika

½ teaspoon freshly ground black pepper

1 teaspoon salt

Preheat oven to 425°F. Cut each potato in half lengthwise. Cut each half, lengthwise, into 4 equally sized wedges. Add the potato wedges to a large mixing bowl with the rest of the ingredients. Toss meticulously to coat the potatoes evenly.

Line a sheet pan with foil. Place the potato wedges, skin side down, on the foil. Be sure to space evenly, so they cook uniformly.

Bake for 35 to 40 minutes, or until well-browned, crusty-edged, and tender. Serve immediately, sprinkled with more salt, if desired.

cornbread

This moist, crumbly version of America's oldest bread has a slight sweetness that makes it a perfect match for spicy foods. A warm, freshly cut wedge next to a steaming bowl of chili is a truly beautiful thing.

serves 6

½ cup unsalted butter, melted

²/₃ cup sugar

2 large eggs

1 cup buttermilk

½ teaspoon baking soda

½ teaspoon salt

1 cup all-purpose flour

1 cup yellow cornmeal

Preheat oven to 375°F. In a large mixing bowl, whisk together the melted butter and sugar. Add the eggs; whisk until combined. Add the buttermilk and baking soda; whisk to combine. Add the flour, cornmeal, and salt. Using a spatula stir until just blended. Do not mix any longer than necessary.

Lightly grease a 10-inch cast iron skillet with butter. (Or you may use a 10-inch square cake pan.) Pour in the batter and bake for about 35 minutes, or until a tester inserted in the center comes out clean. Let cool for at least 15 minutes before serving.

crispy onion rings

Japanese breadcrumbs, called Panko, are available in most large supermarkets, and when combined with this simple batter, produces onion rings so crispy, they defy the laws of nature.

serves 8-10

½ cup all-purpose flour

¼ cup cornstarch

2 tablespoons instant mashed potatoes

big pinch of cayenne

1 cup cold club soda

2-3 cups panko (Japanese-style breadcrumbs), or as needed

fine salt to taste

vegetable oil for frying

2-3 yellow onions, cut into ¼-inch rings

Sift together the flour and cornstarch. Add the instant mashed potatoes, cayenne and club soda. Whisk to combine. Let sit in the fridge for 10 minutes. Meanwhile, heat vegetable oil to 350 degrees F. Pour the breadcrumbs into a shallow dish.

Remove batter from the fridge and check for consistency. The mixture should resemble a slightly thick pancake batter. More club soda can be added to adjust. Working in batches, use a fork to coat the onion rings in the batter, let the excess drip off, and then toss in the panko to coat on both sides.

Fry for about 2-3 minutes, turning over in the oil halfway through, until crispy and golden brown. Drain on a rack, and serve warm, sprinkled with salt.

Note: Regular breadcrumbs can be used, but the panko makes for a much crispier onion ring.

cheesy broccoli gratin

You'll forget all about how nutritious fresh broccoli is when you see this crispy, bubbling, golden-brown beauty coming to the table.

makes 6 portions

¼ cup butter

¼ cup flour

2 cups cold milk

Pinch of nutmeg

Pinch of cayenne pepper

1 teaspoon fresh thyme leaves, chopped (optional)

1 cup (8 ounces) shredded extra-sharp cheddar cheese,

½ teaspoon salt, or to taste

2 pounds (6 cups) fresh broccoli crowns, cut into 2-inch pieces

½ cup plain breadcrumbs

2 tablespoons melted butter

2 tablespoons grated Parmesan cheese

Preheat oven to 375°F. Melt the butter in a saucepan over medium heat, and add the flour. Cook, stirring, for about 3 minutes (the mixture should begin to smell like cooked piecrust). Slowly whisk in the cold milk. Continue whisking until there are no visible lumps. Add the nutmeg, cayenne pepper, and thyme. The sauce will thicken as it comes back to a simmer. Reduce the heat to low, and simmer, stirring occasionally, for 10 minutes.

Turn off the heat, and stir in the cheese. When all the cheese has melted into the sauce, season with salt, and reserve until needed.

Note: Sauce may be strained if you are concerned about lumps.

Bring a pot of salted water to a rapid boil. Add the broccoli and cook for about 5 minutes, or just until the stem ends begin to get tender. Do not overcook, as the broccoli will cook further in the oven. Drain very well (otherwise the gratin will be watery). Transfer to a large mixing bowl.

Pour the cheese sauce over the broccoli, and fold with a spatula until the broccoli is completely coated with the sauce. Transfer into a lightly buttered 2-quart casserole dish, using the spatula to distribute evenly. In a small bowl combine breadcrumbs, butter, and Parmesan. Sprinkle evenly over the top, and oven-bake for 25 minutes, or until the top is browned and bubbly.

creamy corn custard

This corn custard recipe is light, but still rich and satisfying. Since it's so soft and creamy, texturally, it makes a great match for things like barbecue pork ribs, grilled steaks, and fried fish.

serves 8

3 cups corn kernels, fresh, or thawed frozen

1½ cups heavy cream

½ cup milk

1¼ tsp salt

Pinch of cayenne

3 egg yolks

4 eggs

Butter as needed

8 (6 oz) oven-proof ramekins, buttered

Pre-heat oven to 325°F.

Add the corn, cream, milk, salt, and cayenne to a saucepan. Bring to a simmer over medium heat. Turn off heat and remove to cool slightly. Carefully pour into a blender and puree until very smooth. Reserve.

Add the eggs and egg yolks to a mixing bowl and whisk for 30 seconds. Slowly, a cup at a time, stir in the warm corn custard mixture. When everything is combined, ladle the mixture into 8 well buttered, 6 oz ramekins.

Fill a roasting pan or casserole dish with 1-inch of hot water and place in the filled ramekins. Bake for 35 minutes, or until the corn custard is just set. Remove from the baking dish and let cool for 15 minutes before serving.

May be eaten out of the ramekins – or run a paring knife around the inside, and turn over on to a plate for a "fancier" presentation.

steakhouse creamed spinach

This is the king of the steakhouse side dishes. It's not a real steak dinner unless there's creamed spinach on the table.

serves 4-6

½ cup unsalted butter

24 oz pre-washed, ready-to-use baby spinach

½ onion, finely diced

1 whole clove

3 cloves garlic, very finely minced

1/3 cup flour

1½ cups cold milk

Pinch freshly ground nutmeg

Salt and pepper, to taste

Put a large stockpot over high heat. Add 1 tbsp of the butter, and as soon as it melts, dump in all the spinach and cover quickly. Leave for one minute, uncover, and continue cooking, stirring the spinach with a long wooden spoon, until just barely wilted. Transfer to a colander to drain.

When the spinach is cool enough to handle, squeeze as much liquid out as possible, and roughly chop. Press between paper towels to draw out the last of the water, and reserve until needed.

Melt the rest of the butter in a saucepan over medium heat. Add the onions and cook for about 5 minutes, or until translucent. Whisk in the flour and cook for 3 minutes, stirring. Add the garlic and cook for 1 minute. Pour in the cold milk, whisking constantly, and cook until it comes to a simmer. Reduce heat to low and simmer for another 5 minutes. The sauce will thicken as it cooks.

Season the sauce with nutmeg, salt and fresh ground black pepper to taste. Add the spinach, and stir to combine. The dish is ready to serve as soon as the spinach is heated through. Taste once more, and adjust seasoning before serving.

index

macaroni and cheese 76
maple-brined roast pork loin with mustard glaze 60
mushrooms
    chicken and mushroom marsala over garlic toasts 58
    chicken pot pie 68
    classic tuna noodle casserole 70
    cream of mushroom soup 14
    hunter's chicken 62
mussels: san francisco cioppino 22

new england clam chowder 12

okra: chicken and sausage gumbo 38
onions: crispy onion rings 86

parsnips: yankee pot roast 50
pasta & noodles
    classic tuna noodle casserole 70
    macaroni and cheese 76
peas
    chicken pot pie 68
    classic tuna noodle casserole 70
pork
    barbecued baby back ribs 48
    "chili verde" green pork stew 28
    maple-brined roast pork loin with mustard glaze 60
    roast pork tenderloin with black cherry sauce 56
    split pea with ham 10
potatoes
    corn and clam chowder 18
    corned beef and cabbage 66
    garlic and herb steak fries 82
    hearty beef stew 26
    new england clam chowder 12
    scalloped potatoes 80
    yankee pot roast 50

rice: jambalaya 32

salmon: wild salmon cakes with tarragon aioli 72
salsa: "chili verde" green pork stew 28
san francisco cioppino 22
sausage
    chicken and sausage gumbo 38
    jambalaya 32
    shrimp
    chicken and sausage gumbo 38
    jambalaya 32
san francisco cioppino 22
sloppy joes 46
split pea with ham 10

steakhouse creamed spinach 92

texas lone star chili 30
tomatoes
    chicken and sausage gumbo 38
    chicken and white bean chili 36
    cream of tomato soup 8
    firehouse chili con carne 34
    hunter's chicken 62
    jambalaya 32
    king ranch chicken casserole 42
    san francisco cioppino 22
    texas lone star chili 30
tortillas: king ranch chicken casserole 42
tuna: classic tuna noodle casserole 70

yankee pot roast 50